A Mother's Promise

By Katy Newton Naas

Illustrated by Tawny Henson

A Mother's Promise

by Katy Newton Naas

Illustrated by Tawny Henson

A Mother's Promise © 2021 by Katy Newton Naas. All rights reserved. No portion of this book may be reproduced, stored in a retrieval system, or transmitted in any form or by any means, except for brief quotations in printed reviews, without prior permission from the author.

ISBN: 978-1-7340627-7-9

To my boys, Aven and Brayson, my greatest treasures in this world. – K.N.N.
To my children, Alex and Chloé. You are my love and my inspiration. – T.H.

We are so thankful God chose us to be your mothers.

When I held you, I knew you were sent from above.
The smallest gift filled me with the biggest love.

The whole world came to life when
I heard your first cry.

The fireflies lit up for you. The stars danced in the sky.

The snow had more sparkle. The sun had more shine.

The rain made you giggle and I thanked God you were mine.

The flowers bloomed brighter. The birds sang a sweeter song,

and I knew I would love you my whole life long.

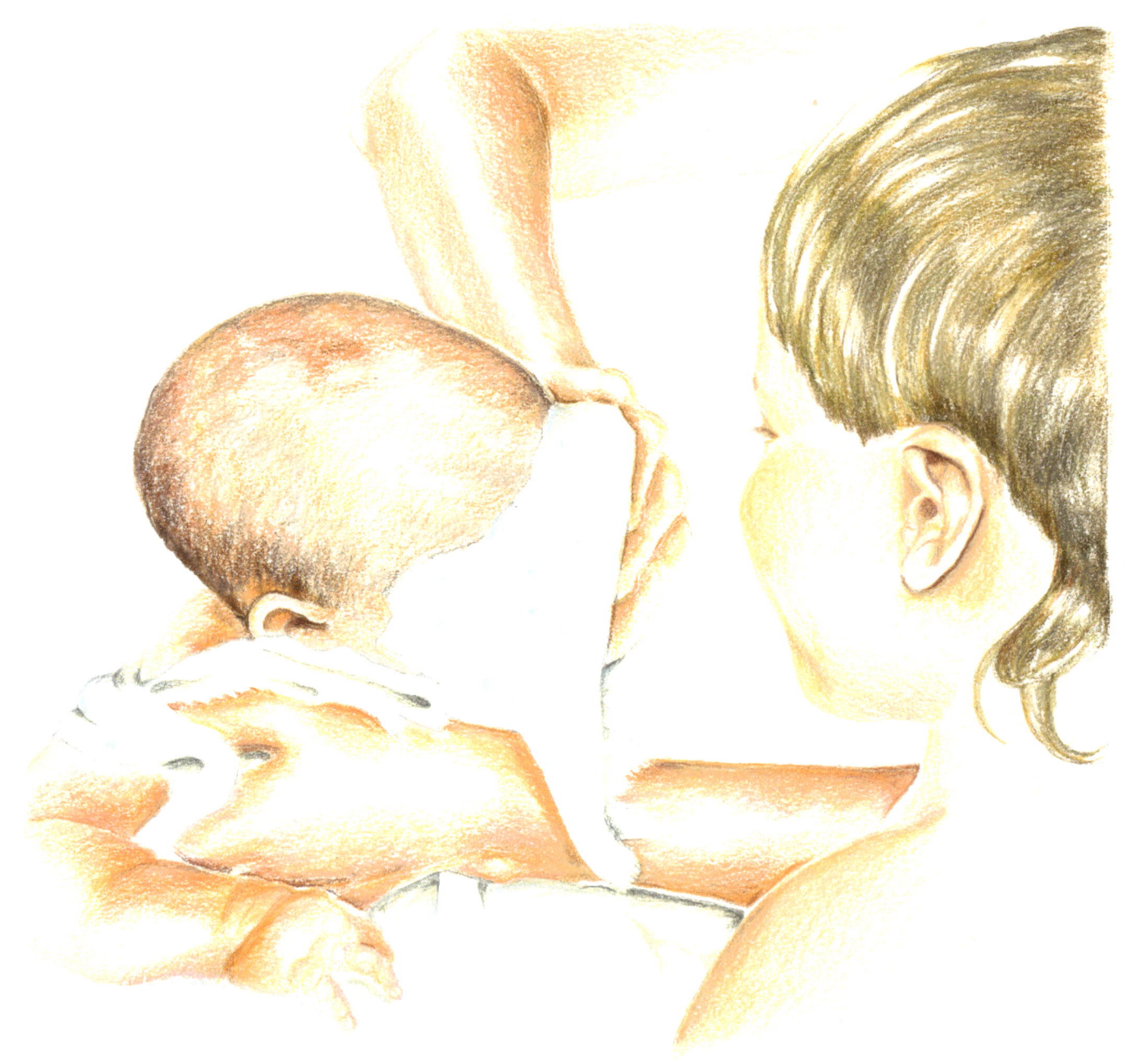

Those first days passed quickly. You grew and you grew.

But as you got bigger, my love for you did, too.

I'll be your shelter when it starts to storm.

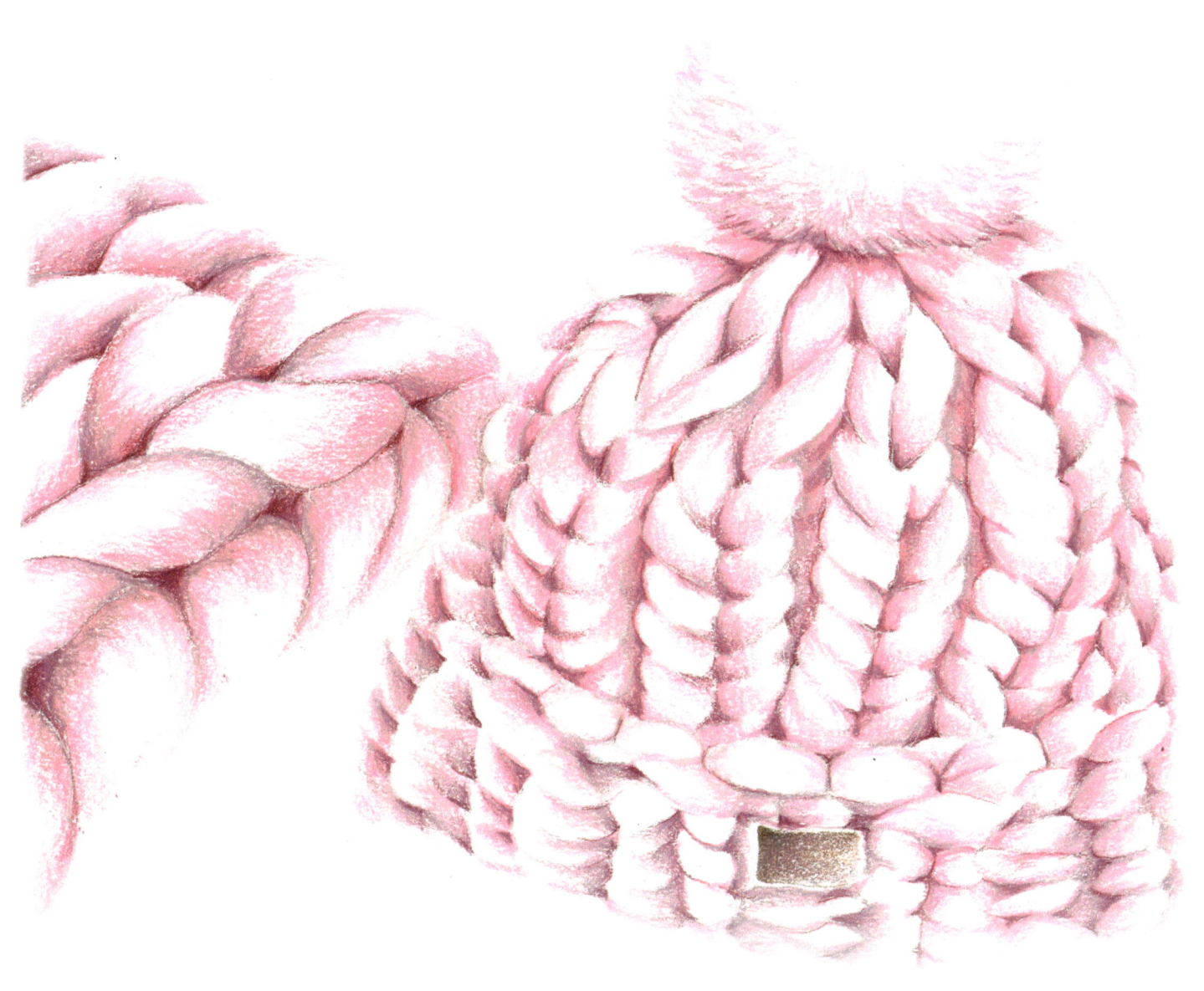

When it's cold outside, I'll be your snuggly and warm.

When you tell jokes, I'll laugh.

When you share secrets, I'll listen.

When you tell stories, I'll watch your eyes light up and glisten.

When your load gets too heavy, I'll carry it for you.

When you get too tired, I'll carry you, too.

I'll be your cheerleader on your biggest day.

When the tears come, I'll be there to wipe them away.

I'll give you the world, take you where you want to go...

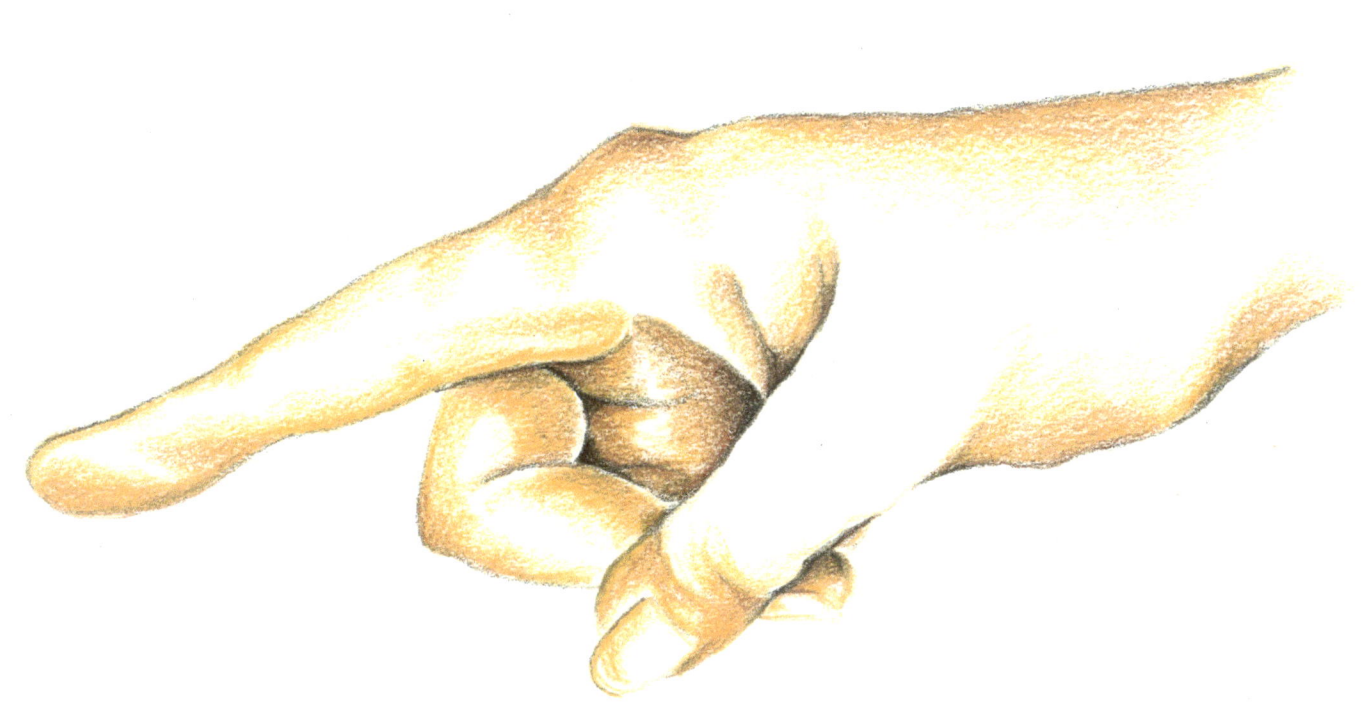

...but know there will be times when I will say *no*.

When you mess up (and you will), I will correct and guide,

but no matter what, I will be by your side.

I'll help you soar as you chase your dreams.

I'll hold you when things fall apart at the seams.

No matter the music, I'll ask you to dance.

I'll hold your hand every time I get the chance.

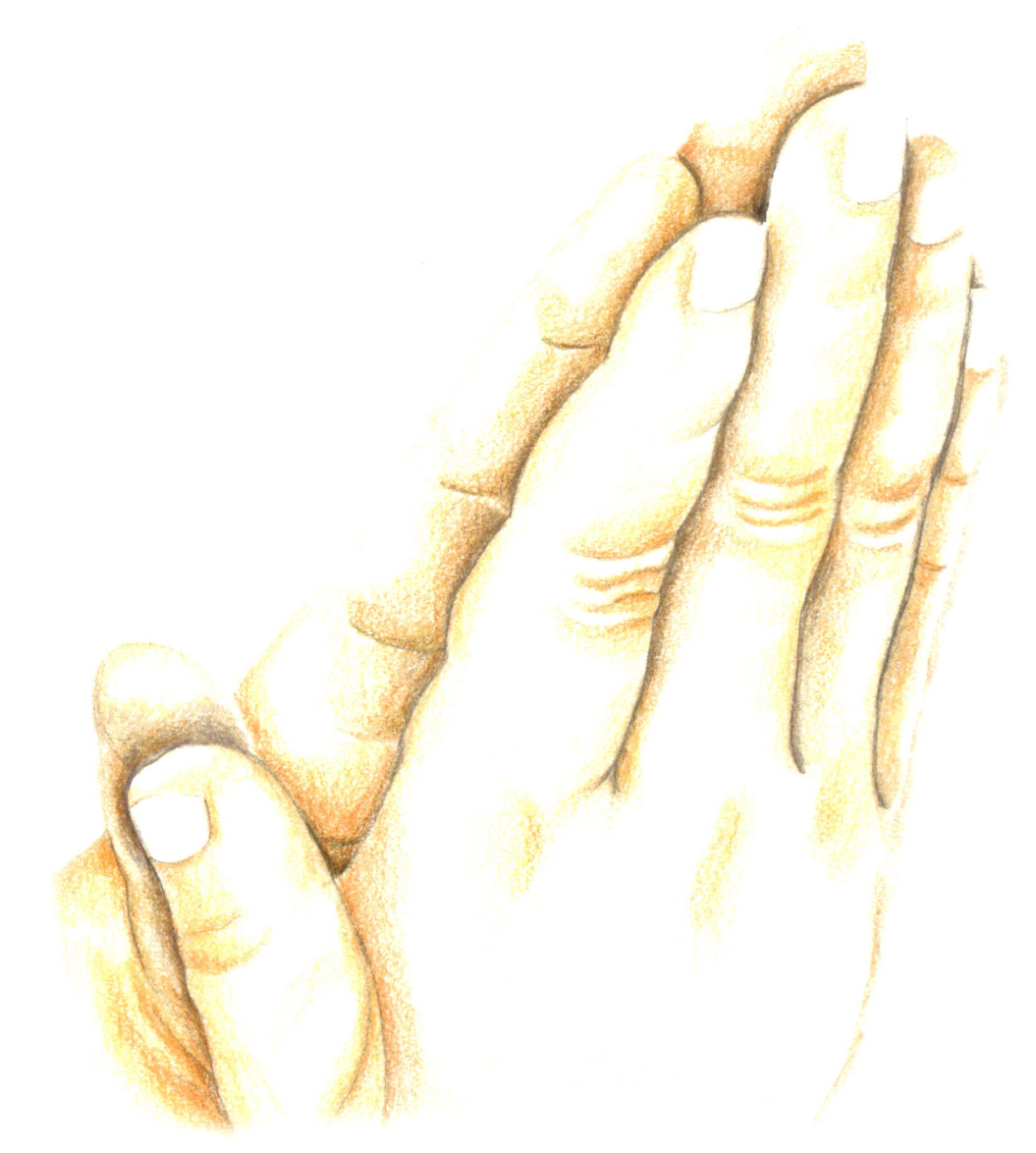

I'll dream with you, plan with you, but most of all,
I'll pray

that you'll trust God to lead you each
step of the way.

Life will take you on adventures, but no matter where,

you can be sure I will always be there.

About the Author

Katy Newton Naas spends most of her free time chasing her two young boys, three dogs, four cats, and thirteen ducks. She has published many books for children, young adults, and adults, including YA Christian Book of the Year Award-winning novel, *Healing Rain*, and Literary Classics International Book Gold Award-winning middle grade novel, *Guardian*. She enjoys serving as youth leader in her church and teaching middle school reading and language arts in the local public school system. Find her and her books at https://www.etsy.com/shop/BooksbyKNN.

About the Illustrator

Tawny Henson is a retired high school art teacher. Tawny has a double Bachelor of Science degree in Design and Illustration and Family and Consumer Sciences from Southern Illinois University. She has two grown children and resides in southern Illinois with her husband.

www.ingramcontent.com/pod-product-compliance
Lightning Source LLC
Chambersburg PA
CBHW040025050426
42452CB00003B/133